What people are saying about
Chew on Things – It Helps You Think: Words of Wisdom from a Worried Canine:

"Entertaining and life-changing...Pets like Casey can help you heal!"

—Andrew Weil, MD
Best-selling author of *Eight Weeks to Optimum Health* and *Healthy Aging*

"*Chew on Things* is a book for dog lovers, lovers of life, and especially for those who are trying to love life. Canine Casey offers fresh, poignant, funny, and accessible wisdom — and helps us celebrate not only life's pleasures, but also its cycles of birth and death. A must-read for children of all ages!"

—Sandy Hogan, Professional Certified Coach and Certified Integral Coach

"Like Casey, our animals live in the now, always follow their hearts, and delight in the joy of every new day...a state of being that inspires us all to live just as fully!"

—Dr. Kenneth R. Pelletier, author, *The Best Alternative Medicine: What Works? What Does Not?*
Clinical Professor of Medicine, University of Arizona College of Medicine and
University of California at San Francisco School of Medicine

"Loving relationships between kindred souls create special gifts. In this loving tribute to Casey, Dr. Iris Bell shares these gifts of genius and compassion with us all. I have known this admirable scientist and wise healer for over twenty years...and now we discover a source of her brilliance."

—Steven Gurgevich, PhD, coauthor (with Joy Gurgevich) of *The Self-Hypnosis Diet*
www.healingwithhypnosis.com

"What an easy, fun to read book with great life lessons. We learn from the animals what we can't seem to learn from each other. Everyone needs at least one Casey in his or her life."

"Nothing makes me laugh like Casey's hard-won truths. As someone who comes from a long line of human worrywarts, I appreciate his genius: 'Worrywarts live longer—we stay out of harm's way—both real and imagined.' *Chew on Things – It Helps You Think* is a loving, reassuring companion through the absurdities of daily life."

"Honor your own uniqueness. Casey's message is lovingly delivered, but Casey's wisdom is not all warm and fuzzy dog breath. Life is hard, life is scary—life happens. Casey knows, and Casey will help you know, and cope, too."

"I knew Casey. He lived life to its fullest. He energetically reminded me of the joys of exploring, cuddling, pondering, and yes, chewing. And he trained his owner so well that she captured some of his 'woo-woo' wisdom and playfulness in this thoroughly enlightening and endearing book. Be prepared for smiles."

WISDOM IS WHERE YOU FIND IT

There are a number of popular books on discovering wisdom in mundane or unexpected places. This one is a little different.

Play when you're young ... and when you're old.

For one thing, it has photographs — wonderful photos — of the four-legged fretful philosopher ... and sometimes his friends.

I'm warm and fuzzy and play a lot. He's a pig.
Need I say more?

For another, seeing things from the puppy point of view gives you a whole new perspective on life and living and loving.

Even if you're afraid of the world,
at least explore your neighborhood.

It's the loving, possibly, that makes this book so special. It is so obviously a labor of love that you can't help but get a healthy dose of it no matter which page you turn to. As Casey puts it,

Be wary of letting people in or out of your life,
but love them to pieces when they are there.

If you love dogs, if you love people, if you love discovering life's lessons in delightful doggy bite-sized pieces, then chew on what you find in here.

CHEW on THINGS – It Helps You Think

Words of Wisdom from a Worried Canine

CHEW on THINGS – It Helps You Think

Words of Wisdom
from a Worried Canine

as told to **Dr. Iris Bell**

Foreword by **Casey B. Worrywart, Dogtor of Philosophy**

CREATIVE
BOOKWORM
PRESS

A Casey B. Worrywart™ Book

Copyright © 2007 Creative Bookworm Press, a Division of Creative Bookworm, LLC

Creative Bookworm Press
9121 East Tanque Verde Road, Suite 105, Tucson, AZ 85749
Ph. 800-214-8110 • FAX 520-749-4509
www.creativebookworm.com • Email: clientservices@creativebookworm.com

Printed in Hong Kong on acid-free paper.

Publishers Cataloging-In-Publication
Bell, Iris.
    Chew on things--it helps you think : words of wisdom from a worried
canine / as told to Iris Bell. -- Tucson, AZ : Creative Bookworm
Press, c2007.
      p. ; cm.
ISBN 13: 978-0-9791653-2-0
ISBN 10: 0-9791653-2-6
    "Foreword by Casey B. Worrywart, Dogtor of Philosophy."
    1. Dogs--Pictorial works. 2. Philosophy. 3. Quality of life. I. Title.

SF430 .B45 2007   2006910454
636.7/0022/2--dc22   0702

Book consultant: Ellen Reid
Cover and book design: Patricia Bacall

To Casey, who knew how to play ball,
on his own terms.

F O R E W O R D

Some dogs have attitude. Some are just goofballs. As a canine, I see myself more along the lines of a soulful fellow. Living life in your own way takes some watching, some worrying, some thinking, and some doing. Now that I've watched, worried, thought, and done things, I want to share what I've learned.

I've learned that you can have lots of adventures, even in your own backyard. Some adventures are fun (like chasing lizards), and some are scary (like seeing your own reflection in the patio glass door). I've learned to be open to whatever comes up and cope with it the best I can.

For those of you who are fellow worriers, hang in there. The way I see it, worrywarts live longer — we stay out of harm's way … both real and imagined. But, eventually, reality shows up and drives the worries away. And then we create new worries. It's a cycle. In the end, it's all about Life — living it every day the best we can and having fun doing it.

So I hope you enjoy my little book. I am quite a character —
and I've loved my life. Maybe it will help you enjoy yours a
little more. But that's up to you — I won't worry about it.

 Casey B. Worrywart, Dogtor of Philosophy

P R E F A C E

Casey wasn't just any special dog. He wasn't just any old furball. Casey was the eccentric, deep, and funny philosopher-king of the window seat and the backyard. This little book is a way to share the life lessons he taught me and everyone who spent time in his presence. He was a dog of few words but many insights into how to puzzle about life and grow in the process.

I got Casey because I wanted a companion animal, a hypoallergenic dog that didn't shed. I chose his breed because I wanted to laugh more. Just looking at a picture of a shaggy soft-coated wheaten terrier, an Irish farm dog, made me smile. One of the dog books I read said that wheatens are the clowns of the dog world. Sounded like a good fit. I wanted a puppy version to be sure to laugh a long time with him. And so I did.

My co-workers threw me a puppy shower just before I drove with a friend to northern Arizona to pick the puppy up at 10 weeks of age from his breeder's kennel. He was a war baby — the first Gulf War — so the breeder sold him to me at a discount. I must have hyperventilated the whole way there out of nervousness and anticipation at becoming a new dog adoptive mom — but he hyperventilated all the way back.

Especially when the car broke down and he was in his new crate in the shade at the gas station, sitting up, peering out through the crate, shifting from paw to paw and looking very worried as only he could do. What kind of an idiot mom had he drawn? One who couldn't even check her car's fan belt before setting out on such an important trip? (Mental note: Train her quickly and surely. *And so he did.*)

Casey lived with me for 14½ years in three different houses and through many changes in both our lives. The breeder told me that his litter arrived early, unexpected and unattended one night during a storm, and the puppies got scattered all over the place, trying to find their birth mother. A very scary beginning, all alone. In the end, Casey died among family and vet staff, held by the people who came to love and admire him for his quirks, his stoicism through illness and paralysis, and his will to live four years longer than the two days the experts had predicted when he was diagnosed with autoimmune hemolytic anemia. A sad ending, as endings tend to be, but not a scary one.

We had each found someone to tolerate our respective worst neurotic traits and extreme moments. True friends. He left a legacy of funny and meaningful insights. This book, including quotes from human thinkers who resonate with Casey's window-seat view on the world, offers his photos and ponderings for his fellow worriers and other types of people to chew over.

Iris R. Bell, MD, PhD
Tucson, Arizona

I think dogs are the most amazing creatures; they give unconditional love.
For me they are the role model for being alive.

— Gilda Radner

... it's all about Life — living it every day the best we can and having fun doing it.

– Casey B. Worrywart

I started out as a puppy. I was very nervous. Mom had to help me get over my fears of rocks little by little in the narrow wash bed of rocks that went across the middle of our backyard. Eventually I felt safe enough to run all over the yard. But you can't run free until you can jump over the wash, over hurdles.

One day I tried a different way of relating to rocks. I ate a lot of very small rocks in the backyard and had to go to the emergency vet. Important lessons:

1) Life has hurdles — make them as scary as you need to so that you have something important to overcome, but …

2) Don't eat your way through them.

My life has been full of terrible misfortunes, most of which never happened.

– Michel de Montaigne

Keep at it until you figure out what you are meant to be. Everyone needs a sense of purpose in life.

The purpose of life is a life of purpose.

– Robert Byrne

When in doubt, hyperventilate.

When really in doubt, hyperventilate more.

To conquer fear is the beginning of wisdom.
– Bertrand Russell

When really really really in doubt, drink water. Lots of it.

Experts say that drinking eight glasses of water a day is very healthy for you. I prefer wide-mouthed bowls instead of glasses, but you get the idea.

Drinking water gives you time to think things through when you are not sure what to do next. Very useful tactic.

If you're going through hell, keep going.
– Winston Churchill

Get advice when you need it.

I once saw a fortune teller at a Humane Society event. Got me going on a whole new way of looking at the world.

The psychic task which a person can and must set for himself is not to feel secure,
but to be able to tolerate insecurity.

– Erich Fromm

Bark when you want to play ball. And don't give up until you get to play. I prefer to woo-woo rather than arf-arf. But it's a matter of personal style.

If a man does not keep pace with his companions, perhaps it is because he hears a different drummer. Let him step to the music which he hears, however measured or far away.

– Henry David Thoreau

Bad hair days come with life. Worry about other things.

With bad hair days, you can just wait them out. Eventually you figure out how to fix it … the hair and the day.

Reality is the leading cause of stress among those in touch with it.

– Lily Tomlin

Play when you're young. And when you're old.

It may be that all games are silly. But then, so are humans.

– Robert Lynd

Sport is a preserver of health.

– Hippocrates

The dog was created specially for children. He is the god of frolic.

– Henry Ward Beecher

Chew on things. It helps you think.

*Then there is the further question of what is the relationship of thinking to reality.
As careful attention shows, thought itself is in an actual process of movement.*

– David Bohm

Put up with your siblings. Sometimes you can shift the blame to them.

Siblings are the people we practice on, the people who teach us about fairness and cooperation and kindness and caring — quite often the hard way.

– Pamela Dugdale

There's always someone smarter than you — deal with it.

It's not that I'm so smart, it's just that I stay with problems longer.

– Albert Einstein

Also, try to play well with everyone. Sometimes it's the best way to go. Everyone has his or her special place in the universe.

I'm warm and fuzzy and play a lot. He's a pig. Need I say more?

You don't get harmony when everybody sings the same note.

– Doug Floyd

New things are scary. Approach with caution. But approach.

It's fear of the unknown. The unknown is what it is. And to be frightened of it is what sends everybody scurrying around chasing dreams, illusions, wars, peace, love, hate, all that — it's all illusion. Unknown is what it is. Accept that it's unknown and it's plain sailing. Everything is unknown — then you're ahead of the game. That's what it is. Right?

– John Lennon

To fetch or not to fetch. Personally, I like chasing the ball, but I don't see any point to bringing it back. They have golden retrievers or labs for that. From my point of view, once you've caught it, you're done. Move on to the next ball. No point in taking it back to the beginning. Life keeps moving forward. So should you.

There are no laurels in life … just new challenges.

– Katharine Hepburn

My favorite movie character was Chance the Gardener in *Being There*. He was just matter-of-fact, in the moment, no pretense. Chance was my role model. I, too, like to watch. And the windows got bigger and bigger as we moved from house to house.

Look out the window. You can see things.

I like to watch.

– Chance the Gardener (Peter Sellers), from the movie *Being There*

31

have always had a pretty good profile, even when I got older. My breeder had considered keeping me to show in the ring. But, rumor has it that my biological father was an outlaw (Mom told me that later in my life, when I could deal with it better) — he got disqualified once for nipping a judge. So, I come from nervous stock. On the bright side, I come by my nervousness honestly.

Parents are the last people on earth who ought to have children.

– Samuel Butler

Stand back if you're not sure about something new. Change is worrisome. But it keeps happening. Eventually you need to go into the room.

Not everything that is faced can be changed, but nothing can be changed until it is faced.

– James A. Baldwin

Rest up often. It's good for the soul and other body parts.

Life is something to do when you can't get to sleep.

– Fran Lebowitz

The world is made up of owners and ownees. Most of us are ownees.

Pick your owner wisely. Train him or her well.

When you make a commitment to a relationship, you invest your attention and energy in it more profoundly because you now experience ownership of that relationship.

– Barbara De Angelis

You can do it if you don't know you can't. Think about it.

Start small and work up to it. I pulled out the drip system for watering the plants one little piece at a time. Finally, I found the big feeder hose underground and played tug of war with it. What a great day!

Don't be afraid to give your best to what seemingly are small jobs.
Every time you conquer one it makes you that much stronger.
If you do the little jobs well, the big ones will tend to take care of themselves.

– Dale Carnegie

Be earnest in everything you do.

In God's world, for those who are in earnest, there is no failure. No work truly done, no word earnestly spoken, no sacrifice freely made, was ever made in vain.

– Frederick W. Robertson

Don't let anyone stop you once you have your sights set on where you want to go.

The question isn't who is going to let me; it's who is going to stop me.

– Ayn Rand

Hang with your friends sometimes. It helps to watch and ponder with them too.

Lots of people want to ride with you in the limo, but what you want is someone who will take the bus with you when the limo breaks down.

– Oprah Winfrey

Expect the best from people, especially if they give you broccoli or flowers to eat.

Health is the greatest gift, contentment the greatest wealth,
faithfulness the best relationship.

– Buddha

Even if you're afraid of the world, at least explore your neighborhood.

I myself ran away from home three times in my life — or so Mom saw it. I only got a little way up the street or across the street each time, but it sure got Mom hysterical when she caught up with me.

The first time was on Christmas Eve, just before my first birthday. The door opened as some guests were leaving, so I just trotted out into the night. Being a creature of habit, of course, I went along the side of the road in the same direction that we took walks. Mom came running and caught up with me — hysterical as she tends to be sometimes — grabbed me by the tail and pulled me off the road just before a car came flying around the corner. She just couldn't settle down and enjoy the night air. Dragged me back home. I could have done without the histrionics. It was such a beautiful night under the stars.

To learn something new, take the path that you took yesterday.

– John Burroughs

My second great adventure on my own was on moving day, New Year's Day, from our second house. It was too small there; the yard just wasn't enough fun. I got out the front door in all the confusion and almost went up the ramp into the moving truck. But, gosh, there was a whole world across the street to see. So, I kept going. Don't let them tell you otherwise — the grass is greener in the other fellow's yard.

When you come to a fork in the road, take it.
– Yogi Berra

My last escape to freedom happened on Cinco de Mayo from our third house. This time, they left the big side gate open by mistake. Granted, I couldn't walk very well by then. But they took off my diaper and my collar because of the rash on my neck. I was free at last! I needed a boost to stand up by Mom's bedside in the AM, but once I got on level ground, off I tottered. They found me several houses down the street, sniffing the flowers. It is always a good thing to stop and sniff flowers. They say that's a cliché, but it's a good one.

Not all those who wander are lost.
– J.R.R. Tolkien

Just a few safety tips for worrywarts:

1) Do not eat poison mushrooms. They make you very sick.

2) Don't mistake a rattlesnake for a new friend. I did. He bit me. I got very, very sick.

3) Don't let them dress you up in funny clothes very often.

Are we having fun yet?

– Bill Griffith

Strangers are worrisome. Make a scene if you can't cope.

When you come to the end of your rope, tie a knot and hang on.

– Franklin D. Roosevelt

Be wary of letting people in or out of your life, but love them to pieces when they are there.

Where there is love there is life.

– Mohandas Gandhi

Read a lot. I do. And keep reading. You learn things. You never know what. The meaning gets deeper and deeper the longer you look at the words.

"Tell me what you read and I'll tell you who you are" is true enough,
but I'd know you better if you told me what you reread.

– François Mauriac

As you get older, let the young ones follow you around. They might learn something.

I believe that every human soul is teaching something to someone
nearly every minute here in mortality.

– M. Russell Ballard

Look outward for pointers, but inward for strength.

It is never too late to be who you might have been.
– George Eliot

There's the inside and the outside. You always want to be in one of those places.

You don't lead by pointing and telling people some place to go.
You lead by going to that place and making a case.

– Ken Kesey

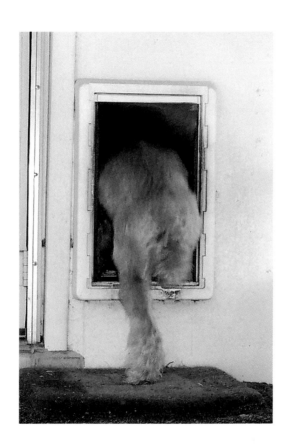

Stay in school.

They give you ribbons when you graduate. Not sure what use they are, but they seem to make moms very happy and proud.

Unlike any other time in our history, we have to know that staying in school and getting an education is the most important thing you can do.

– Alexis Herman

69

Be obedient when you're in obedience school, but for heaven's sake, not when you are out of school. You'll never get anywhere otherwise.

The fastest way to succeed is to look as if you're playing by other people's rules, while quietly playing by your own.

– Michael Korda

Get a good formal name for yourself, for special occasions and to make your family feel proud.

My official AKC name, for instance, is Canyon Thunder.

You can call me Casey. But I also answer to "Hey! Stop that!"

Actually, I have always been afraid of thunder, myself. Thunder sounds like God is very angry, and I can't be sure that it isn't at me. I trembled a lot in my youth … and my old age.

The name of a man is a numbing blow from which he never recovers.

– Marshall McLuhan

Actually, my name, Casey, is really cool. It comes from an Irish surname that was derived from *Ó Cathasaigh,* meaning "descendent of Cathasaigh." The name *Cathasaigh* means "vigilant" in Gaelic.

Others may sleep. I watch. Vigilant … that's me.

It takes courage to grow up and become who you really are.

– e.e. cummings

If you really want to go nuts, try chasing your own shadow.

Sometimes you can't even see it, but you just know it's there, hiding behind you. Other times, your shadow just seems to stay one step ahead of you, no matter what you do.

At least it keeps you company when things get scary.

Most of the shadows of this life are caused by standing in our own sunshine.
– Henry Ward Beecher

Mom thinks that Yogi Berra (the legendary New York Yankee catcher and Mets manager) is a great American philosopher, which is saying a lot — because she grew up in Boston and always roots for the Red Sox. Still Mom says that I'm pretty good at this wisdom business, too.

All the world's a stage and most of us are desperately unrehearsed.

– Sean O'Casey

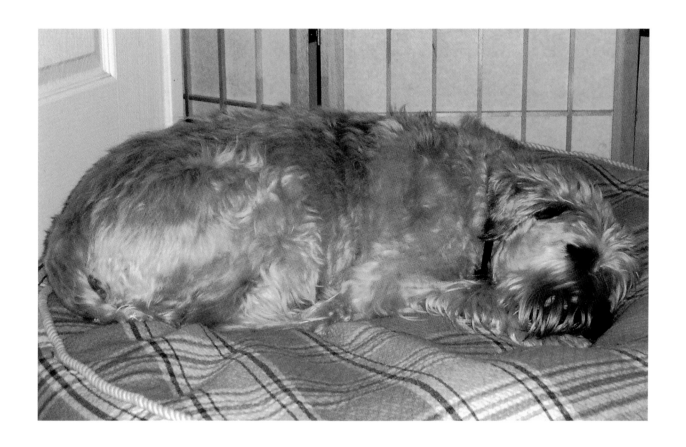

Put up with ribbons, bows, antlers, and other stuff once a year during the holidays. It's a people thing. They really seem to need it.

There's nothing sadder in this world than to awake Christmas morning and not be a child.

– Erma Bombeck

Besides, at holiday time, you get good stuff. I, for example, often get lots of balls that I won't be fetching. Having choices is a great thing … although *making* choices is a bit harder, but worth it in the end.

… Everything can be taken from a man but one thing; the last of the human freedoms —
to choose one's attitude in any given set of circumstances, to choose one's own way.

– Viktor E. Frankl

Explore your world to its edges. However near or far they might be. There's usually something on the other side of the edge that's running just out of reach ... but only for the moment.

We live in an age of universal investigation,
and of exploration of the sources of all movements.

– Alfred de Vigny

Be a character — makes life much more interesting.

Be who you are and say what you feel, because those who mind don't matter
and those who matter don't mind.

– Dr. Seuss

The individual has always had to struggle to keep from being overwhelmed by the tribe.
If you try it, you will be lonely often, and sometimes frightened. But no price is too high
to pay for the privilege of owning yourself.

– Friedrich Nietzsche

Things happen. Keep watching.

Observation is an old man's memory.

– Jonathan Swift

*The power of accurate observation is commonly called cynicism
by those who have not got it.*

– George Bernard Shaw

This getting older business is a challenge. I think that they should put a warning label on age.

It ain't over till it's over.

– Yogi Berra

To sum up, for fellow worriers and other nervous types, watch until you know where you want to go. Then you'll have the nerve to get on your way when your chance comes. When it does, don't let it pass you by.

"Would you tell me, please, which way I ought to go from here?"
"That depends a good deal on where you want to get to," said the Cat.
"I don't much care where — " said Alice.
"Then it doesn't matter which way you go," said the Cat.

– Lewis Carroll, in *Alice's Adventures in Wonderland*

Predetermine the objectives you want to accomplish. Think big, act big,
and set out to accomplish big results.

– Mark Victor Hansen

ACKNOWLEDGMENTS

It took a talented professional team to bring the initial vision of this book from first draft to its wonderful published reality, including Marie LaVigne, Laren Bright, Patricia Bacall, and Brookes Nohlgren. I am especially grateful for the seasoned hand of book shepherd, Ellen Reid, in guiding the process at each step, with her deep knowledge, insight, appreciation of possibilities, and commitment to revisiting and revising the work until each page was truly ready.

Many thanks to those who saw in Casey, the dog who could get into your heart, even if he sometimes nipped at your hand out of uncertainty and fear. They include the dedicated veterinarians, both conventional (Robert Hoge, DVM) and holistic (Diana Bochenski, DVM CVH; Paula Medler, DVM MMQ; Christina Chambreau, DVM), who saved his life at several different times of crisis. And to his devoted human friends Willow Sibert, who saw him so lovingly through his final years and days, and Jane Gersmeyer, who helped raise him from a pup; his acquaintance, Carol Baldwin, who saw something deep in his soul; groomer and wheaten terrier devotee, Kathy Clarke; and his dog/dog-person trainer, Karyn Garvin. Each person helped me help him and supported us through good times and bad.

Loved ya, Puppy-Boy. Rest easy.

RESOURCES FOR CANINE WORRIERS

Becker, Marty, DVM. *Why Do Dogs Drink Out of the Toilet? 101 of the Most Perplexing Questions Answered About Canine Conundrums, Medical Mysteries and Befuddling Behaviors.* HCI, 2006.

McConnell, Patricia, PhD. *For the Love of a Dog: Understanding Emotion in You and Your Best Friend.* Ballentine Books, 2006.

Owens, Paul, and Norma Eckroate. *Dog Whisperer: A Compassionate, Nonviolent Approach to Training.* 2nd ed., 2007; and Paul Owens. *The Dog Whisperer: Beginning and Intermediate Dog Training.* DVD, 2004.

Parsons, Emma. *Click to Calm: Healing the Aggressive Dog* (Karen Pryor Clicker Book). Sunshine Books, 2004.

Rugaas, Turid. *On Talking Terms With Dogs: Calming Signals.* Dogwise Books, 2nd ed., 2005.

Wilde, Nicole, CPDT. *Help for Your Fearful Dog: A Step-by-Step Guide to Helping Your Dog Conquer His Fears.* Phantom Publishing, 2006.

Iris Bell, MD, PhD, is a psychiatrist and university professor. She has written scores of papers on topics ranging from psychiatry to biofeedback to alternative medicine. Dr. Bell has a deep understanding of the human psyche. She teaches, writes, and lives in Tucson, Arizona, with her three dogs — Rosie, Harry, and Charlie.

Creative Bookworm Press is an independent publisher of books, ebooks, audio, video, and related products on pet humor/inspiration and self-help/alternative medicine. Our mission is to entertain, enrich, and expand the hearts, minds, and lives of our readers through high-quality print and other media products.

Our company policy is to donate a portion of the proceeds of all sales of books and products to support non-profit organizations working in fields of importance to our main genres (i.e., animal rescue charities for pet-related sales, and homeopathic education and research charities for alternative medicine–related sales).

To order more copies of *Chew on Things – It Helps You Think: Words of Wisdom from a Worried Canine* and to learn more about our other books and products, we invite you to visit us at:

www.creativebookworm.com

F R E E   B O N U S   G I F T S

As a purchaser of *Chew on Things – It Helps You Think: Words of Wisdom from a Worried Canine*, you are entitled to several special bonus gifts from the author, Dr. Iris Bell.

Visit the bonus page on the Creative Bookworm Press website as listed below and sign up for immediate access to:

- ❧ A downloadable copy of the official Casey B. Worrywart Woe-Is-Me Rating System™ for coping with your worries.

- ❧ Weekly inspirational, fun messages of canine wisdom from Casey B. Worrywart, Dogtor of Philosophy (and some human thinkers), delivered to your email box with his words and photos, to remind you to play (ball, life, and other games) on your own terms as often as possible.

- ❧ A downloadable tips booklet on how Casey's fellow human worrywarts can learn multiple strategies to overcome worries without drugs.

- ❧ And much, much more!

To download your free bonus gifts, go to:

www.chewonthingsbonus.com

www.irisbell.com